SUPER
SANDCASTLE
Super Simple Cooking

Super Simple
Desserts

Easy No-Bake Recipes for Kids

Nancy Tuminelly

Consulting Editor, Diane Craig, M.A./Reading Specialist

ABDO
Publishing Company

Published by ABDO Publishing Company, 8000 West 78th Street, Edina, Minnesota 55439. Copyright © 2011 by Abdo Consulting Group, Inc. International copyrights reserved in all countries. No part of this book may be reproduced in any form without written permission from the publisher. Super SandCastle™ is a trademark and logo of ABDO Publishing Company.

Printed in the United States of America, North Mankato, Minnesota
052010
092010

 PRINTED ON RECYCLED PAPER

Editor: Katherine Hengel
Content Developer: Nancy Tuminelly
Cover and Interior Design and Production: Colleen Dolphin, Mighty Media
Photo Credits: Colleen Dolphin, iStockphoto (Tammy Bryngelson, DarDespot, malerapaso, Dawna Stafford), Shutterstock
Food Production: Colleen Dolphin, Katherine Hengel

The following manufacturers/names appearing in this book are trademarks: Target® Aluminum Foil, Reynolds® Cut-Rite® Wax Paper, Pyrex® Measuring Cup, Proctor Silex

Library of Congress Cataloging-in-Publication Data
Tuminelly, Nancy, 1952-
  Super simple desserts : easy no-bake recipes for kids / Nancy Tuminelly.
    p. cm. -- (Super simple cooking)
Includes bibliographical references and index.
ISBN 978-1-61613-384-9 (alk. paper)
  1. Desserts--Juvenile literature. 2. Quick and easy cookery--Juvenile literature. I. Title.
  TX773.T78 2010
  641.8'6--dc22
                        2009053188

Super SandCastle™ books are created by a team of professional educators, reading specialists, and content developers around five essential components—phonemic awareness, phonics, vocabulary, text comprehension, and fluency—to assist young readers as they develop reading skills and strategies and increase their general knowledge. All books are written, reviewed, and leveled for guided reading, early reading intervention, and Accelerated Reader® programs for use in shared, guided, and independent reading and writing activities to support a balanced approach to literacy instruction.

Note to Adult Helpers

Helping kids learn how to cook is fun! It is a great way for them to practice math and science. Cooking teaches kids about responsibility and boosts their confidence. Plus, they learn how to help out in the kitchen! The recipes in this book require very little adult assistance. But make sure there is always an adult around when kids are in the kitchen. Expect kids to make a mess, but also expect them to clean up after themselves. Most importantly, make the experience pleasurable by sharing and enjoying the food kids make.

Symbols

 knife
Always ask an adult to help you cut with knives.

 microwave
Be careful with hot food! Learn more on page 5.

 nuts
Some people can get very sick if they eat nuts.

Contents

Let's Cook!

The recipes in this book are simple! You don't even need an oven or stove! Cooking teaches you about food, measuring, and following directions. It's fun to make good food! Enjoy your tasty creations with family and friends!

Bon appétit!

Cooking Basics

Before You Start...

- Get permission from an adult.
- Wash your hands.
- Read the recipe at least once.
- Set out all the ingredients, tools, and equipment you will need.
- Keep a towel close by for cleaning up spills.

When You're Done...

- Cover food with plastic wrap or **aluminum** foil. Use containers with tops when you can.
- Put all the ingredients and tools back where you found them.
- Wash all the dishes and **utensils**.
- Clean up your work space.

THINK SAFETY!

- Ask an adult to help you cut things. Use a cutting board.
- Clean up spills to prevent accidents.
- Keep tools and **utensils** away from the edge of the table or countertop.
- Keep potholders or oven mitts close to the microwave.
- Use a sturdy stool if you cannot reach something.

Using the Microwave

- Use dishes that are microwave-safe.
- Never use **aluminum** foil or metal.
- Start with a short cook time. If you need to, add a little more.
- Use oven mitts when removing something.
- Stir liquids before and during heating.

How to Melt Chocolate in the Microwave

Microwave the chocolate for 30 seconds. Using oven mitts, take it out and stir. Repeat until most of the chocolate is melted. Then you can stir until it is smooth. Be patient! If you overcook the chocolate, you have to start over!

Measuring Tips

Wet Ingredients
Set a measuring cup on the countertop. Add the liquid until it reaches the amount you need. Check the measurement from eye level.

Dry Ingredients
Dip the measuring cup or spoon into the dry ingredient. Scoop out a little more than you need. Use the back of a dinner knife to scrape off the **excess**.

Moist Ingredients
Ingredients like brown sugar and dried fruit are a little different. They need to be packed down into the measuring cup. Keep packing until the ingredient reaches your measurement line.

Do You Know This = That?

There are different ways to measure the same amount.

3 teaspoons = 1 tablespoon

4 tablespoons = ¼ cup

5 tablespoons + 1 teaspoon = ⅓ cup

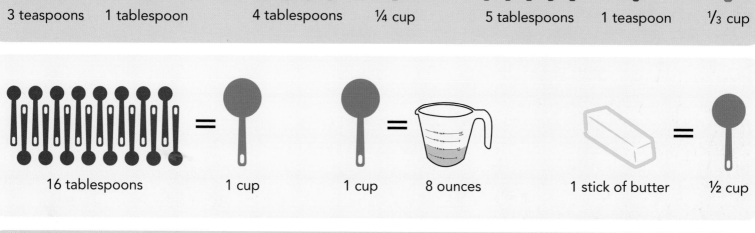

16 tablespoons = 1 cup

1 cup = 8 ounces

1 stick of butter = ½ cup

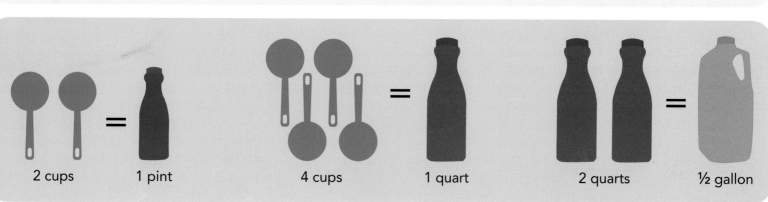

2 cups = 1 pint

4 cups = 1 quart

2 quarts = ½ gallon

Cooking Terms

Chop
Cut into very small pieces with a knife.

Cream
Beat together until smooth with a hand mixer.

Drain
Remove liquid using a strainer or colander.

Melt
Heat something solid until it is **softened**.

Mix

Combine ingredients with a mixing spoon.

Peel

Remove fruit or vegetable skin. Use peeler if needed.

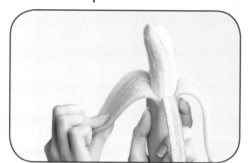

Slice

Cut into thin pieces with a knife.

Spread

Make a smooth layer using a spoon, knife, or spatula.

Keeping Food Fresh

Storing Food

Use **airtight** containers. They have tight lids to keep air out. Plastic zip top bags are good airtight containers too.

Covering Food

Use plastic wrap to cover food going in the refrigerator or on the countertop. Be careful not to put the plastic wrap on too tight. It can stick to your topping!

Tools

Here are some of the tools that you'll need to get started.

baking sheet

oven mitts

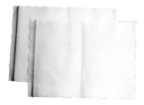

large zip top bags

microwave-safe mixing bowls

9-inch pie pan

cake platter or plate

bundt cake or angel food cake pan

9 x 13-inch baking dish

plastic wrap

wax paper

aluminum foil

mixing spoon

can opener

toothpicks

measuring cup
(wet ingredients)

whisk

dinner spoons

hand mixer

rolling pin

silicone spatula

measuring cups
(dry ingredients)

sharp knife

strainer

fork

measuring spoons

11

Ingredients

Baking Aisle

- [ ] vanilla extract
- [ ] maple-flavored extract
- [ ] 3-inch graham cracker mini crusts
- [ ] 9-inch graham cracker piecrusts
- [ ] powdered sugar
- [ ] chopped nuts
- [ ] almonds
- [ ] peanuts
- [ ] white chocolate chips
- [ ] semi-sweet chocolate chips
- [ ] instant vanilla pudding mix
- [ ] chocolate frosting

- [ ] large marshmallows
- [ ] sweetened condensed milk
- [ ] packaged caramels
- [ ] chocolate-flavored almond bark

Canned Goods

- [ ] 10-ounce can cherry pie filling
- [ ] 20-ounce can crushed pineapple, drained

Frozen

- ☐ frozen whipped topping
- ☐ apple juice concentrate

Dairy

- ☐ cream cheese
- ☐ butter
- ☐ milk

Cookies & Candy

- ☐ graham crackers
- ☐ gumdrops
- ☐ candy-coated, chocolate-covered peanuts
- ☐ cream-filled chocolate sandwich cookies
- ☐ vanilla wafers

Cereal

- ☐ crispy rice cereal
- ☐ sweetened puffed wheat cereal

Other

- ☐ lemon juice
- ☐ maraschino cherries
- ☐ creamy peanut butter
- ☐ dried cranberries
- ☐ dried apples
- ☐ cooking oil spray
- ☐ popped popcorn
- ☐ bananas

Cheesecake Tarts

Delightful cheesy cake bites!

Makes 12 servings

Ingredients

8 ounces cream cheese, softened

14-ounce can sweetened condensed milk

1 tablespoon vanilla extract

¼ cup lemon juice

12 3-inch graham cracker mini crusts

Tools

- can opener
- mixing bowl
- mixing spoon
- measuring spoons
- measuring cups
- baking sheet
- aluminum foil

1. Mix **softened** cream cheese and **condensed** milk in large mixing bowl. Stir in vanilla **extract**.

2. Add lemon juice about 1 teaspoon at a time. Stir well after adding each teaspoon.

3. Spoon mixture into crusts. Set tarts on a baking sheet. Cover with **aluminum** foil and **chill** for at least 4 hours.

 Try almond extract instead of vanilla.

15

Peanutty Butter Bites

Scrumptious morsels!

Makes about 100 pieces

Ingredients

- 1½ cups graham cracker crumbs (about 35 crackers)
- 3½ cups powdered sugar
- 1½ cups creamy peanut butter
- 1 cup butter, melted
- 12 ounces semi-sweet chocolate chips

Tools

- large zip top bag
- rolling pin
- measuring cups
- large mixing bowl
- small mixing bowls
- oven mitts
- mixing spoon
- 9 x 13-inch baking dish
- spatula
- sharp knife

1. Put graham crackers in zip top bag. Use rolling pin to crush crackers into medium-sized crumbs.

2. Mix crumbs, sugar, and peanut butter in a large mixing bowl.

3. Put butter in microwave-safe bowl. Microwave for 20 seconds. Add 10 seconds if needed. Repeat until melted.

4. Stir butter into cookie crumb mixture. Press mixture into baking dish.

5. Put chocolate chips in microwave-safe bowl. Microwave on high for 30 seconds. Using oven mitts, remove and stir. Repeat until melted. Spread chocolate over the peanut butter mixture.

6. **Chill** until chocolate is hard. Cut into bite-size pieces.

Banana Split Pie

A fun and fast dessert!

Makes 6-8 servings

Ingredients

2 cups vanilla wafers

½ cup butter, melted

½ cup butter, softened

8 ounces cream cheese, softened

2 cups powdered sugar

2 bananas, peeled

20-ounce can crushed pineapple, drained

8-ounce container frozen whipped topping, thawed

cherries and chopped nuts

Tools

• measuring cups
• large zip top bag
• rolling pin
• microwave-safe mixing bowls
• mixing spoon
• oven mitts
• 9-inch pie pan
• hand mixer
• strainer
• plastic wrap
• sharp knife

1. Put vanilla wafers in zip top bag. Use rolling pin to crush into crumbs.

2. Put butter in microwave-safe bowl. Microwave for 20 seconds. Add 10 seconds if needed. Repeat until melted.

3. Mix cookie crumbs with melted butter in medium bowl. Press into pie pan to make crust.

4. In large mixing bowl, cream **softened** butter and cream cheese. Add powdered sugar 1 cup at a time. Cream until smooth. Spread mixture over crust.

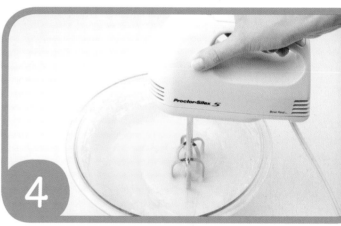

5. Drain pineapple and put over cream cheese mixture. Slice bananas and place over pineapple.

6. Spoon whipped topping over bananas. Sprinkle with chopped nuts. Cover and **chill** for 2 hours before serving.

Maple Cranberry Drops

Yummy desserts!

Makes 36 cookies

Ingredients

2 cups white chocolate chips

¼ cup creamy peanut butter

2 teaspoons maple-flavored extract

3 cups crispy rice cereal

1 cup dried cranberries

Tools

• baking sheet

• wax paper

• measuring cups

• microwave-safe bowl

• oven mitts

• mixing spoon

• measuring spoons

• two dinner spoons

1 Cover baking sheet with wax paper.

2 Put white chocolate chips and peanut butter in a microwave-safe bowl. Microwave on high for 30 seconds. Using oven mitts, take out and stir. Repeat until chocolate chips are melted.

3 Stir in maple **extract**. Then stir in rice cereal and cranberries.

4 Using two dinner spoons, place spoon-sized scoops of mixture onto wax paper. It is important to do this quickly while mixture is still soft. Let stand until firm.

Candy Apple Treats

It's like eating a caramel apple!

Makes 24 bars

Ingredients

cooking oil spray

8 cups sweetened puffed wheat cereal

1½ cups dried apples (cut into half circles)

½ cup roasted almonds or peanuts, chopped (optional)

14 ounces of packaged caramels, unwrapped

6 tablespoons apple juice concentrate, thawed

Tools

- 9 x 13-inch baking dish
- measuring cups
- mixing spoon
- large mixing bowl
- microwave-safe bowl
- oven mitts
- measuring spoons
- silicone spatula
- wax paper
- sharp knife

1. Spray baking dish lightly with cooking oil.

2. Mix cereal, dried apples, and nuts together in large mixing bowl. Set aside.

3. Put caramels and thawed apple juice concentrate in microwave-safe bowl. Microwave on high for 30 seconds. Using oven mitts, take out and stir. Repeat until caramels are melted.

4. Use **silicone** spatula to quickly add melted caramels and apple juice to cereal mixture. Stir until well coated.

5. Pour into prepared pan. Put wax paper on top, and then press mixture evenly. **Chill** for 30 minutes or until firm. Cut into bars.

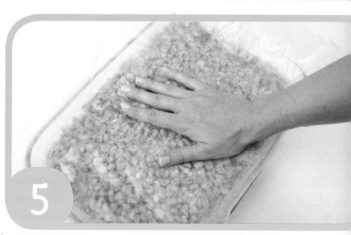

Merry Cherry Surprise

You'll be glad you made two!

Makes 12-16 servings

Ingredients

10-ounce can cherry pie filling

14-ounce can sweetened condensed milk

15-ounce container frozen whipped topping, thawed

2 9-inch graham cracker piecrusts

Tools

• can opener
• large mixing bowl
• mixing spoon
• toothpicks
• aluminum foil

1. Mix pie filling, **condensed** milk, and whipped topping together in large mixing bowl.

2. Pour even amount of mixture into each crust. Use mixing spoon to smooth out the top.

3. Place several toothpicks in each pie. Cover with **aluminum** foil and **chill** in freezer for at least 2 hours. Remove toothpicks before serving.

 Try lemon, peach, or blueberry pie filling.

1

2

3

Chocolate Éclair Cake

A creamy, sweet treat!

Makes 14 servings

Ingredients

2 3½-ounce packages instant vanilla pudding mix

8 ounces frozen whipped topping

3 cups skim milk

16 ounces graham cracker squares

16 ounces prepared chocolate frosting

Tools

- measuring cups
- medium mixing bowl
- hand mixer
- mixing spoon
- 9 x 13-inch baking dish
- dinner knife

1. Cream pudding mix, whipped topping, and milk in medium mixing bowl.

2. Line bottom of baking dish with single layer of graham cracker squares.

3. Spread half of pudding mixture over the graham crackers. Add another layer of crackers, then add the rest of pudding mixture. Top with another layer of crackers.

4. Spread frosting over the top. Cover and **chill** for at least 4 hours before serving.

Terrific Truffles

A cookie and candy treat!

Makes 38-40 balls

Ingredients

18-ounce package cream-filled chocolate sandwich cookies

8 ounces cream cheese, softened

10 ounces chocolate-flavored almond bark

Tools

• large zip top bags

• rolling pin

• fork

• large mixing bowl

• baking sheet

• plastic wrap

• microwave-safe bowl

• mixing spoon

• oven mitts

• toothpicks

• wax paper

1. Put cookies in two large zip top bags. Use rolling pin to crush cookies into medium-sized crumbs.

2. Using a fork, mix cookie crumbs and cream cheese in large mixing bowl.

3. Roll mixture into 1-inch balls and put on baking sheet. Cover with plastic wrap and freeze for 2 hours before continuing.

4. Put almond bark in microwave-safe bowl. Microwave on high for 30 seconds. Using oven mitts, take out and stir. Repeat until almond bark is melted.

5. Use toothpick to dip frozen balls in melted almond bark. Place on wax paper to harden. Store finished truffles in **airtight** container and keep in refrigerator.

Pop! Pop! Popcorn Cake

Fun to make and great to eat!

Makes 12-16 servings

Ingredients

cooking oil spray

½ cup butter, melted

32 large marshmallows

16 cups freshly popped popcorn

1 cup gumdrops, no black ones

1 cup candy-coated, chocolate-covered peanuts

Tools

- measuring cups
- large mixing bowl
- microwave-safe bowl
- oven mitts
- mixing spoon
- bundt cake or angel food cake pan
- cake platter or plate
- aluminum foil
- sharp knife

1. Spray bundt cake or angel food cake pan with cooking oil.

2. Put butter and marshmallows in microwave-safe bowl. Microwave on high for 30 seconds. Using oven mitts, take out and stir. Repeat until mixture is melted.

3. Put popcorn in large bowl. Pour marshmallow mixture over popcorn and stir well. Add candy and nuts. Mix together.

4. Use your hands or the back of a spoon to firmly pack the popcorn mixture into the greased pan.

5. Cover the pan with **aluminum** foil to keep it moist. Let sit for 3 to 4 hours until firm.

6. Turn cake pan onto a large **platter** or cake plate. Shake to loosen the cake from the pan. Cut into pieces.

Glossary

airtight – so well sealed that no air can get in or out.

aluminum – a light metal.

chill – to put something in the refrigerator to make it cold or firm.

condensed – very thick because the liquid has been boiled away.

excess – more than the amount wanted or needed.

extract – a product made by concentrating the juices taken from something such as a plant.

platter – a large plate used for serving food.

silicone – a type of rubbery plastic.

soften – to bring to room temperature or make less firm.

utensil – a tool used to prepare or eat food.